Summer Crochet

15 Pretty Crochet Patterns For Babies

Table of content

Introduction

Summer time is here again, and you know you want to re-do your entire wardrobe. Of course, you get busy with that, but that's not enough. You want to make sure everyone in your family is ready to enjoy a comfortable summer, and to do that, you are going to have to re-do your baby's wardrobe as well.

But your baby is growing so fast, and you don't want to spend a lot of money on the things at the store that you know she is going to grow out of before summer is even over. No, you want her to have something that is cute, fashionable, and cool, and that you can enjoy for the time she fits in it.

What better way to do that than to make it yourself? You know how to crochet, so why not take your skills to the next level and create something your baby will love to wear this summer, and will treasure for years to come?

If this sounds like you, then you have come to the right place. In this book, you are going to learn everything you need to know to make your own baby crochet items, ensuring that your lovely little one is going to have everything she needs to stay cool and fresh this summer, with you right there by her side.

Grab your yarn and your favorite crochet hook and settle in.

Let's get started.

The Patterns

Pretty as a Poppy Striped Sun Dress

You will need 1 skein of yarn per color you choose to use and a size J crochet hook.

Change colors suited to your taste, or use the photo as a reference.

Measure around your baby's chest, then chain a length that is equal to this measurement. Join with a slip stitch. Chain 1, turn, and single crochet back to the other side. chain 1, turn, and single crochet back to the beginning. Chain 1, turn, and single crochet back to the other side.

Next, begin the skirt.

Chain 5, skip the first stitch, and join with a slip stitch into the next stitch. Chain 5, skip the next 3 stitches, and join with a slip stitch into the next stitch. Chain 5, skip the next 3 stitches, and join with a slip stitch into the next stitch. Join with a slip stitch when you get back to the beginning.

For the next row, you are going to chain 6, and join with a slip stitch into the chain space. Chain 6, and join with a slip stitch into the next chain space. Chain 6, and join with a slip stich into the next chain space. Repeat around. You are going to notice an increase with this, so continue with this pattern until the skirt is as long as you want it to be. Tie off, and add a scalloped hem.

Chain 1, and single crochet in the first stitch, then double crochet in the next stitch 3 times. Single crochet in the next stitch, then double crochet in the next stitch 3 times. Single crochet in the next stitch, then double crochet in the next stitch 3 times. Repeat around the row, joining with a slip stitch. Tie off.

Go back to the top of the piece now, and continue with the single crochet until you reach your baby's arm pits. You are then going to increase the size of the row for the sleeves.

Measure as you go, and continue until you have enough sleeves for the dress to stay on. Make sure all is secure, and tie off.

Little Leo Oversized Elf Hat

You will need 1 skein of yarn per color you choose to use and a size J crochet hook.

Measure around your baby's head and chain a length equal to this measurement. Chain 2, and double crochet across the row, joining with a slip stitch. Chain 2, turn, and double crochet back to the other side, joining with a slip stitch. Chain 2, turn, and double crochet across the row, joining with a slip stitch.

Once you are high enough with the brim of the hat, you are ready to start the decrease: this is going to be open worked, but you are going to bring the hat inward and down to a fine point.

Chain 5, skip the first stitch, and join with a slip stitch into the next stitch. Chain 5, skip the next 3 stitches, and join with a slip stitch into the next stitch. Chain 5, skip the next 3 stitches, and join with a slip stitch into the next stitch. Join with a slip stitch when you get back to the beginning.

Skip loops as you work, bringing the hat into a nice point.

Create the tassel using a DVD case, wrapping the yarn around until you have a nice bunch, then cut the yarn. Secure with yarn, and sew to the tip of the hat.

That's it! You are done!

A Beautiful Mess Flower Sun Dress

You will need 1 skein of yarn per color you choose to use and a size J crochet hook.

Measure around your baby's chest, then chain a length that is equal to this measurement. Join with a slip stitch. Chain 1, turn, and single crochet back to the other side. chain 1, turn, and single crochet back to the beginning. Chain 1, turn, and single crochet back to the other side.

Next, begin the skirt.

Chain 5, skip the first stitch, and join with a slip stitch into the next stitch. Chain 5, skip the next 3 stitches, and join with a slip stitch into the next stitch. Chain 5, skip the next 3 stitches, and join with a slip stitch into the next stitch. Join with a slip stitch when you get back to the beginning.

For the next row, you are going to chain 6, and join with a slip stitch into the chain space. Chain 6, and join with a slip stitch into the next chain space. Chain 6, and join with a slip stich into the next chain space. Repeat around. You are going to notice an increase with this, so continue with this pattern until the skirt is as long as you want it to be. Tie off,

Go back to the top now, and continue with the single crochet until you are happy with the rise of the dress. Tie off, then add 2 chains of single crochet for the straps, and create 5 flowers to sew onto the front.

For the flowers:

Chain 4 and join with a slip stitch to form a ring. Single crochet in the center of this ring 10 times, and join with a slip stitch.

Chain 1, turn, and single crochet back to the other side, joining with a slip stitch.

Chain 1, and single crochet in the first stitch, then double crochet in the next stitch 3 times. Single crochet in the next stitch, then double crochet in the next stitch 3 times. Single crochet in the next stitch, then double crochet in the next stitch 3 times. Repeat around the row, joining with a slip stitch.

Tie off, and repeat for remaining flowers.

Sew to the front of the dress, and you are done!

Little Hippy Sun Hat

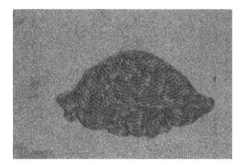

You will need 1 skein of yarn per color you choose to use and a size J crochet hook.

Chain 4 and join with a slip stitch to form a ring. Single crochet in the center of this ring 10 times, and join with a slip stitch.

Chain 1, turn, and single crochet back to the other side, joining with a slip stitch. Chain 1, turn, and single crochet across the row, joining with a slip stitch. Chain 1, turn, and single crochet back to the other side, once again joining with a slip stitch.

Measure on your baby as you work, ensuring you get the proper fit. Decrease slightly as you work, so the hat is going to have some structure for staying in place.

Chain 1, turn, and single crochet in the first 5 stitches, and skip the next stitch. Single crochet in the next 5 stitches, and skip the next stitch. Single crochet in the next 5 stitches, and skip the next stitch. You are going to continue with this until you have reached around the row.

Then, return to your normal single crochet.

Continue with this pattern until the hat is the size you wish, then begin the scalloped edge for the border.

Chain 1, and single crochet in the first stitch, then double crochet in the next stitch 3 times. Single crochet in the next stitch, then double crochet in the next stitch 3 times. Single crochet in the next stitch, then double crochet in the next stitch 3 times. Repeat around the row, joining with a slip stitch. Tie off.

Sunshine and Unicorns Rainbow Baby Blanket

You will need 1 skein of yarn per color you choose to use and a size J crochet hook.

Use the photo as a reference for changing colors – every 6 rows.

Starting with the color of your choice, chain a length that is 5 feet long.

Single crochet across the row. Chain 1, turn, and single crochet back to the other side. Chain 1, turn, and single crochet across the row. Chain 1, turn, and single crochet back to the other side. Chain 1, turn, and single crochet across the row. Chain 1, turn, and single crochet back to the other side. Chain 1, turn, and single crochet across the row. Chain 1, turn, and single crochet back to the other side.

Change colors.

Work 2 rows of white, then go back to a different color.

Single crochet across the row. Chain 1, turn, and single crochet back to the other side. Chain 1, turn, and single crochet across the row. Chain 1, turn, and single crochet back to the other side. Chain 1, turn, and single crochet across the row. Chain 1, turn, and single crochet back to the other side. Chain 1, turn, and single crochet across the row. Chain 1, turn, and single crochet back to the other side.

Change colors.

Work 2 rows of white, then go back to a different color.

Continue until you are happy with the size of the blanket, and tie off. Work 1 row of single crochet in white for the border, and you are done!

Easiest Ever Baby Tunic

You will need 1 skein of yarn per color you choose to use and a size J crochet hook.

Using one of your baby's current shirts, measure from shoulder to shoulder, then add 2 inches. Single crochet a length that is equal to this length.

Single crochet across the row. Chain 1, turn, and single crochet back to the other side. Chain 1, turn, and single crochet across the row. Chain 1, turn, and single crochet back to the other side. Chain 1, turn, and single crochet across the row. Chain 1, turn, and single crochet back to the other side. Chain 1, turn, and single crochet across the row. Chain 1, turn, and single crochet back to the other side.

Continue until this rectangle matches the size of the shirt. This is the back, so now you are going to tie it off and set it aside.

Repeat now, working from the bottom to the top.

Chain a length that is equal to your first length.

Single crochet across the row. Chain 1, turn, and single crochet back to the other side. Chain 1, turn, and single crochet across the row. Chain 1, turn, and single crochet back to the other side. Chain 1, turn, and single crochet across the row. Chain 1, turn, and single crochet back to the other side. Chain 1, turn, and single crochet across the row. Chain 1, turn, and single crochet back to the other side.

When you are nearing the neck, only single crochet in to the front of the shirt to where the neck starts. Chain 1, turn, and single crochet back to the beginning. Chain 1, turn, and single crochet your new row. Chain 1, turn, and single crochet back to the beginning. You are going to continue with this until the piece reaches the shoulder.

Tie off, then join with a slip stitch on the other side, and repeat, forming the other side of the neck. Tie off, and you are ready to assemble.

Hold both pieces together and sew up the sides with a whip stitch. You are then going to work a single crochet border around the base, neck, and arms. Tie off, and you are done!

Keep Up with Me Baby Booties

You will need 1 skein of yarn per color you choose to use and a size J crochet hook.

Chain a length that is 2 inches long, then single crochet across the row. Instead of turning and coming back to the beginning, you are going to continue to single crochet down and around the bottom and back to the beginning from below. Join with a slip stitch.

Chain 1, turn, and single crochet back to the other side, joining with a slip stitch. Chain 1, turn, and single crochet across the row, joining with a slip stitch. Chain 1, turn, and single crochet back to the other side, once again joining with a slip stitch. Chain 1, turn, and single crochet across the row, joining with a slip stitch.

Follow the pattern until the oval can fit beneath your baby's foot. You are then going to work 1 decrease row to shape the shoe.

Chain 1, and single crochet in the first 3 stitches, then skip the next stitch. Single crochet in the next 3 stitches, and skip the next stitch. Single crochet in the next 3 stitches, and skip the next stitch. Single crochet in the next 3 stitches, and skip the next stitch. Single crochet in the next 3 stitches, and skip the next stitch.

Continue around.

Go back to single crochet now as you work your way up the side of the shoe.

Chain 1, turn, and single crochet back to the other side, joining with a slip stitch. Chain 1, turn, and single crochet across the row, joining with a slip stitch. Chain 1, turn, and single crochet back to the other side, once again joining with a slip stitch. Chain 1, turn, and single crochet across the row, joining with a slip stitch.

As you work your way around the toes, decrease to bring the top of the shoe inward. Measure on your baby as you do this to ensure the proper fit.

When you are happy with the size of the shoe, extend the outer end by enough stitches to reach across the top of the shoe, forming a strap across the top. Work 3 rows of single crochet with this, and attach a snap or a button so you can close the shoe. Tie off, and repeat for the other shoe.

That's it! Your baby is ready to step out in style!

The Upsy Downsy Throw

You will need 1 skein of yarn per color you choose to use and a size J crochet hook.

Use the photo as a reference, or just change colors whenever you like. Start with the color of your choice, and chain a length that is 7 feet long.

Single crochet across the row. Chain 1, turn, and single crochet in the first 10 stitches, then skip the next 2 stitches. Single crochet in the next 10 stitches, then skip the next 2 stitches, single crochet in the next 10 stitches, then skip the next 2 stitches. Repeat across the row.

Next, follow the pattern you have just made once more.

Chain 1, turn, and single crochet in the first 10 stitches, then skip the next 2 stitches. Single crochet in the next 10 stitches, then skip the next 2 stitches, single crochet in the next 10 stitches, then skip the next 2 stitches. Repeat across the row.

Now you are going to work normal single crochet, following the pattern you have created with the previous rows.

Single crochet across the row. Chain 1, turn, and single crochet back to the other side. Chain 1, turn, and single crochet across the row. Chain 1, turn, and single crochet back to the other side. Chain 1, turn, and single crochet across the row. Chain 1, turn, and single crochet back to the other side. Chain 1, turn, and single crochet across the row. Chain 1, turn, and single crochet back to the other side.

Remember to change colors every few rows (or stick to your own color scheme.)

When you are happy with the size of the blanket, tie off.

You can create tassels by using a DVD case and your yarn, wrapping the yarn around the DVD case until you have a nice thick set. Snip this off in the middle, then tie the yarn around the center. Secure in place on the blanket, then tie off.

That's it! you are done!

Cloverfield Blanket

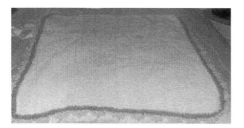

You will need 1 skein of yarn per color you choose to use and a size J crochet hook.

Starting with the color of your choice, chain a length that is 5 feet long.

Single crochet across the row. Chain 1, turn, and single crochet back to the other side. Chain 1, turn, and single crochet across the row. Chain 1, turn, and single crochet back to the other side. Chain 1, turn, and single crochet across the row. Chain 1, turn, and single crochet back to the other side. Chain 1, turn, and single crochet across the row. Chain 1, turn, and single crochet back to the other side.

When you have a square, you are ready to begin the border. Tie off and change to another color, then join with a slip stitch. Single crochet across the row, join with a slip stitch, then tie off.

Change to another color, and you are ready to add the scalloped border.

Join the next color with a slip stitch.

Chain 1, turn, and single crochet back to the other side, joining with a slip stitch.

Chain 1, and single crochet in the first stitch, then double crochet in the next stitch 3 times. Single crochet in the next stitch, then double crochet in the next stitch 3 times. Single crochet in the next stitch, then double crochet in the next stitch 3 times. Repeat around the row, joining with a slip stitch. Tie off.

My Little Molly Hat

You will need 1 skein of yarn in the color of your choice and a size G crochet hook.

Chain 4 and join with a slip stitch to form a ring. Single crochet in the center of this ring 10 times, and join with a slip stitch.

Chain 1, turn, and single crochet back to the other side, joining with a slip stitch. Chain 1, turn, and single crochet across the row, joining with a slip stitch. Chain 1, turn, and single crochet back to the other side, once again joining with a slip stitch. Chain 1, turn, and single crochet across the row, joining with a slip stitch. Chain 1, turn, and single crochet back to the other side, joining with a slip stitch. Chain 1, turn, and single crochet across the row, joining with a slip stitch. Chain 1, turn, and single crochet back to the other side, joining with a slip stitch.

Measure on your baby as you work, ensuring you get the proper fit. Decrease slightly as you work, so the hat is going to have some structure for staying in place.

Chain 1, turn, and single crochet in the first 5 stitches, and skip the next stitch. Single crochet in the next 5 stitches, and skip the next stitch. Single crochet in the next 5 stitches, and skip the next stitch. You are going to continue with this until you have reached around the row.

Then, return to your normal single crochet.

Continue with this pattern until the hat is the size you wish, then tie off.

For the flower:

Chain 4 and join with a slip stitch to form a ring. Single crochet in the center of this ring 10 times, and join with a slip stitch.

Chain 1, turn, and single crochet back to the other side, joining with a slip stitch.

Chain 1, and single crochet in the first stitch, then double crochet in the next stitch 3 times. Single crochet in the next stitch, then double crochet in the next stitch 3 times. Single crochet in the next stitch, then double crochet in the next stitch 3 times. Repeat around the row, joining with a slip stitch. Tie off.

Repeat once more, only this time make the flower larger for the base of the flower.

Sew the smaller flower in place on top of the larger flower, then sew both to the hat, wherever you like. Make sure all is secure, then tie off, and you are done!

The Wide-Brimmed Floppy Brimmed Hat

You will need 1 skein of yarn in the color of our choice and a size G crochet hook.

Chain 4 and join with a slip stitch to form a ring. Single crochet in the center of this ring 10 times, and join with a slip stitch.

Chain 1, turn, and single crochet back to the other side, joining with a slip stitch. Chain 1, turn, and single crochet across the row, joining with a slip stitch. Chain 1, turn, and single crochet back to the other side, once again joining with a slip stitch.

Measure on your baby as you work, ensuring you get the proper fit. Decrease slightly as you work, so the hat is going to have some structure for staying in place.

Chain 1, turn, and single crochet in the first 5 stitches, and skip the next stitch. Single crochet in the next 5 stitches, and skip the next stitch. Single crochet in the next 5 stitches, and skip the next stitch. You are going to continue with this until you have reached around the row.

Then, return to your normal single crochet.

Continue with this pattern until the hat is the size you wish, then tie off.

For the flower:

Chain 4 and join with a slip stitch to form a ring. Single crochet in the center of this ring 10 times, and join with a slip stitch.

Chain 1, turn, and single crochet back to the other side, joining with a slip stitch.

Chain 1, and single crochet in the first stitch, then double crochet in the next stitch 3 times. Single crochet in the next stitch, then double crochet in the next stitch 3 times. Single crochet in the next stitch, then double crochet in the next stitch 3 times. Repeat around the row, joining with a slip stitch.

Sew this flower in place on the hat, wherever you like. Make sure all is secure, then tie off, and you are done!

Green Machine Diaper Cover

You will need 1 skein of yarn per color you choose to use and a size G crochet hook.

Use a diaper that is the size your child is currently wearing, and make a cover that is large enough to encase the outside of the piece. Lay the diaper down, with the inside facing the table and pressed flat.

Chain a length that is equal to the back, and single crochet across the row. Chain 1, turn, and single crochet back to the other side. Chain 1, turn, and single crochet across the row.

Follow the shape of the diaper as you work. As you get to the point that will rest between your child's legs, you need to start adding a decrease into the pattern.

Chain 1, skip the first stitch, and single crochet across the row, skipping the last stitch. Chain 1, skip the first stitch, and single crochet across the row, skipping the last stitch. Chain 1, and skip the first stitch, then single crochet across the row, skipping the last stitch. Repeat this as you continue to work your way down the piece.

Go back to regular single crochet through the bottom, then when you get back to the other side, begin adding an increase.

Chain 1, and single crochet in the first stitch 2 times. Single crochet across the row, and single crochet in the last stitch 2 times. Chain 1, and single crochet in the first stitch 2 times, then single crochet across the row, and single crochet in the last stitch 2 times. Continue to do this as you open up once more, following the shape of the diaper.

When you have the right size, finish the project with a single crochet row around the entire piece.

Tie off, and add buttons, snaps, or ties to keep the cover in place. That's it! You are done!

Going Green Washable Diaper Cloths

You will need 1 skein of yarn per color you choose to use and a size J crochet hook.

Chain a length that is about 8 inches wide. You want there to be plenty of room to give you space for ample cleaning, but you don't want it to be so big that it is cumbersome to use.

Single crochet across the row. Chain 1, turn, and single crochet back to the other side, this time in the front loop only. Chain 1, turn, and single crochet across the row, in the front loop only. Chain 1, turn, and single crochet back to the other side, again in the front loop only. Chain 1, turn, and single crochet across the row, in the front loop only. Chain 1, turn, and single crochet back to the other side, once again in the front loop only. Chain 1, turn, and single crochet across the row, in the front loop only. Chain 1, turn, and single crochet back to the other side, in the front loop only.

Repeat until you have a square, paying attention to your tension as you work up the side of the piece. Tie off, then work 1 row of single crochet around the entire edge as a border. That's it, you are done!

Angel's Kiss Face Cloth

You will need 1 skein of yarn per color you choose to use and a size J crochet hook.

Chain a length that is 6 inches long.

Single crochet across the row. Chain 1, turn, and single crochet back to the other side. Chain 1, turn, and single crochet across the row. Chain 1, turn, and single crochet back to the other side. Chain 1, turn, and single crochet across the row. Chain 1, turn, and single crochet back to the other side. Chain 1, turn, and single crochet across the row. Chain 1, turn, and single crochet back to the other side.

Pay attention to your tension as you work up the side of the washcloth. You don't want it to be too tight and pull in the sides, and you don't want it to be too loose and create gaps.

When you are happy with the size of the piece, tie off. You can finish with a single crochet border, or you can leave it as is.

"Look at Me Mommy!" Flip Flops

You will need 1 skein of yarn per color you choose to use and a size J crochet hook.

Chain 5 and check to ensure that it fits around the strap of the flip flops. Adjust as necessary.

Single crochet across the row. Chain 1, turn, and single crochet back to the other side. Chain 1, turn, and single crochet across the row. Chain 1, turn, and single crochet back to the other side. Chain 1, turn, and single crochet across the row. Chain 1, turn, and single crochet back to the other side. Chain 1, turn, and single crochet across the row. Chain 1, turn, and single crochet back to the other side.

Measure against the flip flops as you go along, making sure that the strip you are creating will fit snuggly against the straps of the flip flops. Once you have reached from the base of the shoe to the top, tie off.

Repeat 3 more times, once for the other half of the flip flop you are currently working on, and 2 times for the other flip flop. When you have all your strips created, take your yarn needle, and sew them around the straps on the flip flops.

Make sure it is a snug fit, and that your covers won't be uncomfortable or slip off the shoe. Tie off, and you are done!

Conclusion

There you have it, everything you need to create a variety of adorable summer patterns for that special little one in your life. You know there is nothing more important to you than making sure your child is safe, secure, and happy, and what better way to do that than to make her something by hand?

I hope this book was able to show you just how easy it is for you to make your own crochet baby items, and that you take what you have learned here and turn it into something amazing. There's no end to the ways you can show off your baby crochet skills, and every time you do, you will see how wonderful these patterns really are.

Dive in with both feet, and give your baby something you are proud of.

Happy crocheting.

Made in the USA
Monee, IL
06 March 2022